NORHAM CAS

NORTHUMBERLAND

Andrew Saunders

A castle was first built at Norham in the twelfth century by a Bishop of Durham. The huge bulk of this building stands on a site of great defensive strength overlooking the River Tweed. It was repeatedly attacked and besieged during the thirteenth and fourteenth centuries, and was captured by the Scots three times between 1136 and 1322. In 1513 it was stormed by James IV and largely destroyed. It was later rebuilt to take into account advances in gunpowder artillery, but had lost its importance as a defensive stronghold by the end of the sixteenth century. The remains of the impressive Great Tower can still reveal signs of four building phases spanning the twelfth to the sixteenth centuries.

This handbook provides a detailed tour of the picturesque remains of the castle, and explains its full and fascinating history.

❖ CONTENTS ❖

Published by English Heritage, 23 Savile Row, London W1X 1AB
© English Heritage 1998
First published by English Heritage 1998, reprinted 2001

Photographs by English Heritage Photographic Unit
and copyright of English Heritage, unless otherwise stated.

Edited by Louise Wilson. Designed by Grahame Dudley Associates.
Printed in England by Sterling
C30, 02/01, FA3517, ISBN 1-85074-700-8

DESCRIPTION AND TOUR

The Great Tower and Inner Ward of the castle seen from the south-west through one of the remaining arches in the south curtain wall

Today's approach to the castle is the same as that used in the sixteenth century, leading through the ramparts of the outer courtyard, known as the Outer Ward, towards the deep-ditched enclosure of the Inner Ward, dominated by the lofty bulk of the Great Tower. The site of the castle was chosen for its natural defensive strength, as it is protected on the north and west by the steep cliff above the River Tweed, and on the east by a deep ravine. The modern road follows much of the course of the outer moat towards the west. There are also remains of an earthwork enclosure in the field to the south, defined by a curving stream fed by the Mill Burn. This suggests that there was a third element to the castle - a barmkin or enclosure for stock. The gatehouse linking the Outer Ward with this enclosure is the aptly named Sheep Gate. A plan by the military engineer Rowland Johnson (1561) also shows a row of houses south of the road (see page 27).

OUTER WARD AND SHEEP GATE

The castle entrance is now through an early nineteenth-century custodian's cottage built into the ruins of one of the towers or bulwarks projecting from the curtain wall. Except on the eastern side of the Outer

Ward, where there is a length of high-standing, twelfth-century masonry, there is, in fact, little left to see of the medieval curtain wall on the crest of the massive rampart. What does remain is a partially complete arcade. Two arches survive to the west of the cottage and further west of the high gate-arch of Sheep Gate are the dressed stone springers for what were four more arches built on stubs of the rubble wall-core of the medieval curtain wall. The arcade is an early sixteenth-century development, probably part of a system of reinforcement (counterforts) within earth banking to front and rear to heighten the rampart. Part of the frontal earth bank can be seen to the east, beyond

the most complete of the surviving bulwarks. The arcade would also have supported a parapet and wall walk. What earth banking there was has largely been removed, leaving the stone arches exposed. We know that this must have happened by the early eighteenth century, as this was when the Buck brothers drew their view of the castle which clearly shows the open arches.

Projecting from the earlier curtain wall are the foundations of at least four rounded towers, probably built in the thirteenth century. These towers were rebuilt as four-sided, pointed towers or bulwarks in the 1520s, following the wholesale destruction caused by the 1513 siege

View of the castle, drawn by Samuel and Nathaniel Buck in 1728. It shows the open arches of the south curtain wall and the Sheep Gate as a tall structure with several floors

THE SOUTH—EAST VIEW OF NORHAM CASTLE.

(see page 24). Only the bulwark to the east of the cottage survives to any extent, with a lower tier of five embrasures, although little of this can now be seen from ground level.

The Sheep Gate, which projects beyond the line of the curtain wall west of the cottage, was probably built early in the thirteenth century. An entrance arch remains and traces of the rounded twin towers flanking the entrance. Beside the gatehouse, the height of the arcade wall is indicated by steeply sloping masonry perhaps forming a parapet. The Buck engraving suggests that the Sheep Gate was a tall structure with two floors over the gate passage. Beyond the Sheep Gate, to the west, are the foundations and paved floor of a building which may have served as a guardroom.

WEST GATE

Once inside the Outer Ward, at the bottom of the steep slope to the left, the remains of the West Gate can be seen. This was the original outer gate to the castle. East of it, a length of high curtain wall overlooks the River Tweed. The West Gate faces the village of Norham and had a complicated history. In the part of it leading into the Inner Ward, remains of the twelfth-century, rectangular gate passage can be seen, divided into two parts by shallow buttress-like pilasters and once vaulted over. Behind the

left-hand jamb of the outer gate is a large socket in the wall face into which a draw-bar would have slotted to prevent the gates from being forced open. Here, as elsewhere in the castle, the twelfth-century masonry can be recognized by its medium-sized squared stones or ashlar, dressed with heavy diagonal tooling and bedded with wide joints.

The gatehouse underwent many repairs and improvements, and the accounts tell that it was rebuilt in 1408. This involved extending the front towards the edge of a re-cut ditch with the grooves for a portcullis behind the new outer gate. On the left, a partial masonry blocking shows that the entrance was later reduced in width. Beyond it were the walls of a short defended approach, or

The West Gate of the castle from the bridge over the moat, with the village in the background

The West Gate from the west showing the defended approach and masonry abutments that once supported a drawbridge

One of the low-level gun embrasures, set at angles in the north curtain wall

barbican, and the masonry abutments for a drawbridge. This gatehouse was badly damaged during the sieges of 1497 and 1513. It was restored in 1520, but in 1554 it was blocked up again, except for a small postern gate cut in the barbican wall. The line of the outer ditch to the south of the barbican has been lost due to the course of the present road. In the ditch to the north is a low cross-wall containing a pistol loop to counter an attack from the direction of the river.

The high curtain wall, extending eastwards from the gatehouse along the cliff above the river, was rebuilt in the fifteenth century and again after 1513. This part of the castle was very vulnerable to bombardment from the Scottish side of the river. In its final phase, the curtain was set out on a series of oblique angles with three low-level embrasures for guns mounted on flat beds, each set on a beam laid in the floor of the embrasures. The guns were operated through small rectangular openings with largely fixed lines of fire. The wall is thick in order to resist bombardment and to carry more guns at a higher level. From its outer face, three wide traverses project to give protection from enemy gunfire. The level of the ground on the inner side of the wall must have been raised, because, on the outside of the wall, there is the arch of a sallyport below what is now internal ground level.

Further east, on the outside of the curtain wall, are the collapsed portions of an early, D-shaped tower which once stood on the outer edge of the inner moat. Inside the Outer Ward, near the West Gate, are the scanty remains of substantial stone buildings of unknown purpose, set on terraces cut into the sloping ground.

THE APPROACH TO THE INNER WARD

Climb up eastwards from the West Gate, approaching the impressively deep ditch or moat that separates the Inner Ward from the rest of the castle.

Along the inner lip of the ditch are the remains of a rampart which survives from the first castle of 1121 - the earth and timber ringwork of Bishop Flambard. The ditch was recut in 1495, when water was led into it through the curtain wall that sealed the moat to the east, by means of Bishop Fox's Aqueduct (see page 16). In the moat bottom you can see the elaborate stone washing floors through which the water had to pass before flowing on through a sluice system built against the northern curtain wall. Alongside is a brewhouse with the base for a brewing vat at one end. The elaborate stone structures in the moat bottom suggest that wool may have been processed here, perhaps providing the bishop with some extra funds to meet the continuous large maintenance bill for the castle. Against the curtain wall at the north

The brewhouse alongside one of the elaborate stone structures in the bottom of the moat, probably used for processing wool

end of the moat, was a multi-storey building, which controlled the sluices and had a long room containing a fireplace above it, and the now missing castle chapel above that. It seems that the room beneath the chapel was converted into stables in the 1520s.

Little remains today of the bridge abutments, barbican and gatehouse that served the Inner Ward. Sufficient original masonry survives to show that it was of twelfth-century date, but whether of Bishop Flambard's construction, or Bishop du Puiset's, cannot be determined. The gatehouse was rebuilt after 1513 and was still roofed in 1561.

GREAT HALL AND CHAMBERS

Cross the modern wooden bridge over the moat to the Inner Ward of the castle.

The principal buildings of the castle were always in the Inner Ward as this was the most secure part. The most distinguished residential elements were in the Great Tower and this was where the bishop and any important guests would be accommodated on the occasions when they were present. On the northern side of the Ward was the public part of the castle, with the Great Hall in the centre, great chamber towards the east, and the service rooms and kitchen at the lower (western) end.

To get to the Great Hall, walk straight ahead of you until the Great Tower is on your right. Here turn left and, passing a well, enter the high end of the hall.

The hall, like those of Oxford and Cambridge colleges today, had many functions, including being a place

Interior of the Great Tower seen from the Great Hall with the well in the foreground

The remains of the oven at the far end of the kitchen

where business was transacted and the ceremonial part of the castle where formal banquets could be served. The hall and chamber complex in its ruined state belongs to the reconstruction of the castle after 1513, but was undoubtedly on the same site as its predecessors.

The Great Hall is a substantial room, 18.3 by 9.1m, (60 by 30ft), with its fireplace in the north wall. Walk towards the far (western) end where the entrance can be seen. This would have led to a passage which gave access to the buttery and pantry on the left hand side and a timber partition on the right, screening the service end from the hall itself. Between the buttery and pantry is a central door which leads into the kitchen. A large fireplace is built into the left-hand wall. At the far end of the kitchen, a large domed oven is built against the back of the

gatehouse. This would have been used for baking bread, pies and pasties. It would also, incidentally, have supplied warmth to the rooms in the gatehouse.

Walk back through the Great Hall, past the fireplace on the left, to the opposite end, where there would have been the dais for the high table. Doorways in the end wall led into a more private room, also heated by a fireplace and with a spiral stair leading up to the Great Chamber. There could have been an additional storey above that. By the sixteenth century the hall had a flat roof to carry guns for firing across the Tweed.

The arrangements behind the Great Chamber are puzzling. The eastern side of the Great Chamber is built against a parallel range of buildings which also abuts the north face of the Great Tower. This four-teenth- or fifteenth-century range of buildings was of high quality, and at its southern end the springers of vault ribs can still be seen on the eastern wall. The range extended northwards, but its eastern wall seems to have collapsed, perhaps another casualty of the sieges. The presumed line of this wall is crossed at an oblique angle by the course of the sixteenth-century curtain wall, producing a very cramped space at the north end. The later curtain wall has windows at several levels for a replacement range of buildings with two storeys of fairly low-grade accommodation contrived at the back of the Great Chamber. At the same time, the former ground floor was filled up to first-floor level to be reached by a straight flight of steps on the south.

There are also the remains of other ranges of buildings constructed against the curtain wall on the south side of the courtyard, opposite the Great Hall and kitchen. The original purpose of these is unclear but the building range immediately south of the gatehouse appears to have been filled up to provide a gun platform as part of the sixteenth-century remodelling.

The Great Tower

The glory of Norham is the Great Tower which, in its ruined state, has been a favoured subject for artists. Many changes of construction can be seen in its masonry fabric, particularly on the inner and outer faces of its south wall. This has led to recent archaeological research which has defined four major phases of building and design that can be supported by historical records. The first phase stems from c.1121 and the first castle of Bishop Flambard; the second from c.1160, being the work of Bishop du Puiset; the third from c.1422–30 and, finally, the reconstruction in 1513–20[1].

Norham Castle, Sunrise, *a painting by JMW Turner*

PLAN OF THE GROUND FLOOR OF THE GREAT TOWER SHOWING THE VARIOUS PHASES OF BUILDING

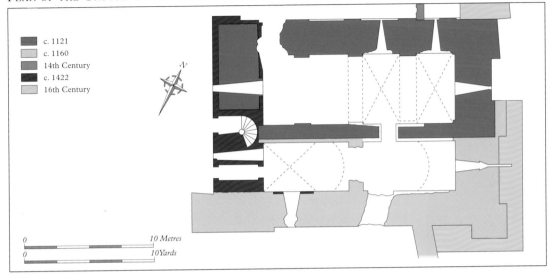

- ██ c. 1121
- ░░ c. 1160
- ▓▓ 14th Century
- ██ c. 1422
- ░░ 16th Century

N

| 0 | 10 Metres |
| 0 | 10 Yards |

UNDERCROFT (GROUND FLOOR)

The first phase is recognised to be the northern half of the Great Tower which has a groin vault to its undercroft, divided by transverse arches, and is distinct from the later barrel vault parallel to it to the south which was divided in two by a cross arch. The external design can be seen at ground level from the shallow pilaster buttresses repeated internally which break the building into bays. Small window loops light the ground floor.

Leave by the door at the west end of this room. Turn left and left again to the doorway in the west wall of the Great Tower and up the spiral stair to the first floor.

This is the fifteenth-century stair. Originally there would have been an external stair to the first floor on the north side.

The groin-vaulted, northern part of the undercroft of the Great Tower

Round-headed window embrasure in the east wall of the Great Tower - part of the second building phase

The ghost of the twelfth-century pitched roof above the large upper window in the east wall of the Great Tower

First floor

The first floor is divided into two by a spine wall. To the left (north) are remains of Bishop Flambard's hall above the groin-vaulted undercroft. It has a bench running along its east wall with a narrow window above. On the north wall a blocked mural passage can be seen.

To the right of the spine wall is a room lit by large round-headed windows in the south and east walls. This is part of the addition to Bishop Flambard's hall built by Bishop du Puiset and differs significantly from the earlier hall to the north. This second-phase structure was extended over the line of the ringwork rampart to the lip of the moat, and it seems that the south wall of the first-phase building was reduced in thickness to become a comparatively thin spine wall, probably to make more floor space. In the vaults below, the form of the southern part differs from east to west and is divided into two by a transverse arch. On the first and second floors, the different phases can be identified by the fact that the round-headed windows in the south and east walls have embrasures much larger than the narrow loops in the walls of the first-phase building.

There is a twelfth-century fireplace in the south wall of the first floor towards the west, and a blocked opening leading to a garderobe or latrine. It has been suggested that Bishop du Puiset added a tower-like private suite of chambers of high quality at the western end of the range, the two floors separated by a groin-vault for which there are hints in the south wall. It is, however, difficult to establish the existence of a closing west wall for this tower. Alternatively, the upper two floors might have extended across over the full plan. The drastic rebuilding of the whole western third of the Great Tower in the fifteenth century has removed much of the evidence and made this a debatable question. What is clear is the ghost of the twelfth-century pitched roof above the large upper window in the east wall. The reconstruction of the western third of the Great Tower in the early fifteenth century removed the earlier pitched roof and heightened the building to make provision for four storeys of high-quality lodgings.

The new lodgings were now reached by the newel stair in the

The base of the garderobe or latrine built in 1429–30 on the south wall of the Great Tower

This fifteenth-century masonry with horizontal string courses, on the external west wall of the Great Tower, contrasts with the uneven ashlar work of the twelfth–century parts

predominantly two-storey residential range over a basement. They required additional sanitation provisions, and a new latrine is accounted for in 1429–30. The remains of this survive as an extension of the south-west angle of the Great Tower and can be seen on the inner slope of the ditch when you leave the Inner Ward and walk round towards the east.

As you descend the spiral staircase, look up and notice how it climbs to the full height of the tower. Standing outside the Great Tower again, and looking at the stonework, the twelfth-century, uneven ashlar walls are distinct from the fifteenth-century masonry, which has horizontal string courses and pointed two-light windows under square hood moulds.

The final phase of building on the Great Tower came following the middle of the west wall which rises to the full height of the tower to serve a central vaulted look-out turret above roof level. This is similar to the central turret of the near contemporary Warkworth Castle. These new lodgings made the Great Tower take on the appearance of a tower house rather than a

*Cutaway drawing of the
Great Tower in the fifteenth
century by Peter Dunn*

damage of the 1513 siege. The
shattered north wall of the Great
Tower may have been patched up,
but the work was so badly done that
it had fallen again by 1551. Only the
southern half of the tower was refur-
bished, its wall tops slightly lowered,
and it was given a flat roof to
provide a gun platform. By the end
of the sixteenth century, however,

the castle was generally badly
decayed and the constable was
forced to live in a few rooms in the
Sheep Gate.

Clapham's Tower

*Walk back towards the moat bridge but,
before crossing it, turn left through an
opening in the south range.*

View of the Great Tower from the west, with the remains of Clapham's Tower in the foreground

This leads to a door into the basement of Clapham's Tower, which projects far beyond the southern wall of the Inner Ward. The tower flanked the approaches to the Inner Ward and would have covered much of the interior of the Outer Ward with gunfire. It was built in 1515 as a piece of artillery fortification and is similar to the bulwarks on the curtain of the Outer Ward. Together they suggest prototypes for angled bastions mounting artillery, such as those adopted at Berwick in the late 1550s, but these at Norham had no true flanking capacity and their defensive effectiveness was therefore limited. What remains of Clapham's Tower is its basement, with a sloping floor following the inner lip of the ditch. A stone vault once carried the first floor. The springing of vault ribs can be seen at its entrance. If the Buck drawing can be relied on, there were probably at least two floors above. The basement contains one gunport covering the ground in front of the Inner Ward gatehouse.

From Clapham's Tower, walk westwards and leave the Inner Ward via the bridge. Here, turn left into the Outer Ward and follow the outside of the moat.

This is an opportunity to look at the

Bishop Fox's Aqueduct: the point at which water was brought into the moat through the east curtain wall to feed the brewery and stone washing floors in the moat bottom. They may have been used for processing wool

full height of the Great Tower and note the differing character of the masonry, particularly that of the twelfth century to the right (east) compared with the larger ashlar of the fifteenth-century addition to the right (west). The lower walling of the latrine turret can be seen at the south-west corner on the inner slope of the ditch with an opening at low level discharging into the moat. Against the south-east corner of the Great Tower are massive buttresses. These, and similar reinforcement along the east side, may relate to the patching-up that followed destruction during sieges, or from basic structural weakness.

Abutting the south side of the Great Tower, is a fifteenth-century wall which crossed the moat and linked with the curtain wall surrounding the Outer Ward. Against the outside of this wall across the moat are the abutments of Bishop Fox's aqueduct, which conducted water from outside the castle through an opening in the wall to serve the washing floors in the bottom of the Inner Ward moat to the west.

At the point where the Outer Ward curtain and the cross wall meet, are the now shapeless ruins of Sandur's Tower. This was a thirteenth-century tower in the same relationship to the inner moat as the ruined tower on its northern side mentioned earlier. Sandur's Tower was partially rebuilt after 1513 on the same angled form as the Outer Ward bulwarks and Clapham's Tower.

Walk back on the inside of the Outer Ward where there is a high stretch of early curtain wall. This is the only surviving length of twelfth-century masonry which can be seen in the Outer Ward. It finishes before you reach the back of the only sixteenth-century bulwark that remains to first-floor level. From here you return to the ticket office.

THE HISTORY OF NORHAM CASTLE

Day set on Norham's castled steep,
And Tweed's fair river, broad and deep,
And Cheviot's mountains lone:
The battlled towers, the donjon keep,
The loophole grates, where captives weep,
The flanking walls that round it sweep,
In yellow lustre shone.

Sir Walter Scott, *Marmion*

The romantic setting for Sir Walter Scott's epic poem, *Marmion*, is based on a story told by Sir Thomas Gray in his book, *Scalacronica*. In this story, the fourteenth-century Lincolnshire knight, Sir William Marmion, as an act of chivalrous devotion to his mistress, volunteered to serve in the most dangerous place in England. This was Norham Castle. He had been given a gold-crested helmet to make known amid glorious dangers. Gray's father, Sir Thomas Gray the elder, was constable of Norham at the time and when a Scottish force appeared before the castle, he called to Marmion, 'Sir Knight, you come here

as a knight errant to make that helm known... there are your enemies: spur on and do battle in the midst of them'. With that, Sir William Marmion rode out to drive off the Scots single-handed, was badly wounded in the process, and was rescued by the garrison led by the constable.

The story well illustrates the situation of Norham Castle as a Border stronghold. It was captured by the Scots on four occasions (1136, 1138, 1322 and 1513) and unsuccessfully besieged by them five times (1215, 1318, 1319, 1327 and 1497). Together with the nearby castles of Berwick and Wark, Norham was an essential part of the defences of the Eastern March (border). Its strategic value in controlling a ford and a well-used crossing point over the Tweed was still a factor in the early sixteenth century, when the castle was remodelled to mount gunpowder artillery. However, like most castles, it was more than a fortress. It was the administrative centre for the Bishop of Durham's most northern territory of Norhamshire and Islandshire, and its palatial qualities provided suitable accommodation for kings as well as bishops and a setting for high diplomacy. Yet, apart from the Great Tower, there is today very little to see of the medieval castle other than its overall plan and the foundations of towers and gatehouses. Today, the standing remains reveal how the castle was rebuilt after being substantially destroyed during its siege and capture in 1513. This made it habitable again, but really converted it into an early Tudor frontier fort

Reconstruction of Norham Castle (1560) showing its strong defensive position. Artist: Peter Dunn

designed for gunpowder artillery.

When civil war broke out in England between Stephen and Matilda, David I of Scotland tried to seize Northumberland in 1136, claiming the earldom to be his by inheritance. He invaded the northern counties again in 1138 in a notoriously atrocious campaign. He was defeated by forces raised by Archbishop Thurston of York and some other northern barons at the Battle of the Standard near Northallerton. In

Depiction of siege warfare in the early fourteenth century. Mordred besieging the Tower of London, Roman du Saint Graal, *Flanders*

The ruins of Berwick Castle from the south

spite of this defeat, David managed to retain Cumberland and Northumberland because of the political weakness of King Stephen, though he held these lands only nominally as a vassal of the English king. In 1157, Henry II forced the Scottish king, Malcolm IV, to give them up, but Malcolm's successor, William the Lion, continued the conflict until his capture at Alnwick in 1174. He was then forced to accept English over-lordship, although still hankering for the earldom of Northumberland. He continued to exploit King John's diffi-culties in 1209, but backed down when John appeared with an army at Norham. When the Treaty of York was later negotiated between the two kingdoms in 1237, Alexander II abandoned Scottish claims to the two northern counties and the Tweed-Cheviot line became an established institution. There followed a temporary period of peace in the Borders.

FOUR HUNDRED YEARS OF RESISTANCE

Throughout this uncertain period, Norham Castle figured prominently in the political events. The castle was founded by Bishop Ranulph Flambard of Durham (1099-1128) in 1121, in order, as a contemporary wrote, to protect his franchise from robbers and Scots. The core of the original castle was the roughly oval

The chancel of St Cuthbert's Church at Norham was rebuilt, like the Castle, by Bishop de Puiset. It is a fascinating example of the romanesque style in Northumberland churches

'ringwork' which is now described as the Inner Ward. Its enclosure would have been faced with timber and backed by an earth rampart with a timber breastwork on top of it. Within this enclosure was a two-storey stone building, probably the bishop's ceremonial hall. The large crescent-shaped Outer Ward and an irregular-shaped enclosure further to the south were also part of the original castle. This castle was soon captured by the Scots during David of Scotland's campaign into Northumberland in 1136, but was returned to the bishop shortly after-wards. Two years later, Norham was again attacked, and this time substan-tially destroyed. After the Battle of the Standard, its site was again returned to the bishop. Thereafter, the castle was taken into royal hands at times when the bishopric was vacant, or

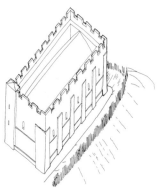

Drawing of the Great Tower in its first phase. Philip Dixon and Pamela Marshall

when kings were doubtful of the bishop's loyalty, but this was always done without prejudice to the rights of the bishop, and it was returned to him when danger had passed.

The strategic importance of Norham was such that, soon after Hugh de Puiset became Bishop of Durham in 1153, he was ordered by Henry II to rebuild the castle, which he did between 1157 and 1170. Bishop du Puiset built lavishly at Durham Castle. He was also responsible for building the chancel of St Cuthbert's Church at Norham, which remains an outstanding example of romanesque architecture among Northumberland parish churches. His work at Norham Castle too was on a grand scale. It involved the building of the Great Tower to provide high-status, private, chambers and incorporated the early two-storey hall. The earliest masonry in the Inner Ward gatehouse and in the West Gate is likely to be part of this rebuilding. King John, between 1208 and 1212, spent large sums on the castle and may have been responsible for building the Sheep Gate and other elements of the Outer Ward.

Alexander II of Scotland unsuccessfully besieged Norham for forty days in 1215. Peace was signed at Norham in 1219 and this lasted along the Border for most of the thirteenth century. The castle continued to be maintained, and some accounts for 1261–62, found recently, show that

the constable repaired the roofs of the chambers over the gatehouses and other buildings. Norham's position, adjacent to the then Scots-held Berwick Castle, gave it a diplomatic as well as military significance. The most noteworthy event in the castle's history occurred in May, 1291. Bishop Anthony Beck entertained Edward I and his advisors at Norham when the king arbitrated between thirteen competitors for the Scottish

The coronation of Edward I depicted in an early manuscript

MICHAEL HOLFLRD

The illluminated Charter of Free Warren attached to the great Seal of England. This was a grant by Edward I to Roger de Pilkington and his heirs of free hunting rights in Lancashire. It is dated 1291 and was sealed at Norham Castle while the king was staying there to settle the dispute over the heir to the Scottish throne

throne (The Great Cause). Edward had asked sixty-seven northern magnates to attend him at Norham with their feudal quotas of armed men. Judgement was made in favour of John Baliol in 1292, at Berwick Castle, and three days later Baliol paid homage to Edward in the church of Norham. The scale of the royal presence was such that 164 horses were required for the royal household at Norham. This total had risen to 269 by the following year, implying that there must have been a wealth of temporary accommodation provided in and around the castle.

Edward I's subsequent claims of overlordship over Scotland pre-cipitated the Scottish War of Independence which led to prolonged warfare and destruction in the Borders. For the Scots, this was to have its high point in the defeat of Edward II's English army in 1314 at Bannockburn. Norham Castle was so strong that it was not attacked during Robert Bruce's invasions of Northumberland in 1311 and 1312. It was besieged in 1318 for almost a year, but although the Outer Ward was captured, it was retaken after only three days. In the following year, there was another siege of the castle, lasting for seven months, and a third in 1322. Norham was eventually seized and taken in 1327 but, following the Treaty of Northampton in the next year, it was restored to the bishop.

There was only slow economic recovery in the Borders after the mid-fourteenth century. When the nobility were in a position to rebuild their homes, the memory of the recent warfare seems to have encouraged them to build tower houses instead of one- or two-storey hall houses. From a military point of view, Norham benefited from this period of relative peace and recovery, and its Great Tower was remodelled to create something resembling a tower house.

We are very fortunate that, from the fifteenth century onwards, there are detailed building accounts for the castle that allow the identification of buildings and their function. In 1408, the West Gate was said to have been 'rebuilt from the ground'. The major development came in 1422–23 when a reference to the building of the 'new' tower within the castle implies the remodelling of the Great Tower to its present form. This was followed in 1429–30 by the addition of the latrine tower on the south side of the building to serve the new lodgings. The castle figured briefly in the Wars of the Roses, when the Lancastrian-held castles of Alnwick and Norham surrendered to the Earl of Warwick in 1464. More repairs were made in

Robert the Bruce at Bannockburn

THE BRIDGEMAN ART LIBRARY

1476 under the orders of Edward IV, to be followed in 1480 by a commission to take bombards and cannon to Norham. This indicates that by this time the castle was capable of mounting gunpowder artillery. Bishop Fox strengthened the castle in 1494 and this was presumably the occasion when the water supply to the inner moat was renewed.

The castle was again unsuccessfully besieged by the Scots in 1497 in support of the pretender for the English throne, Perkin Warbeck. It was the occasion when the celebrated bombard, Mons Meg, was wheeled out of Edinburgh for the siege. The bombardment caused considerable damage and afterwards there was a good deal of improvement to the defences. The two-storeyed West Gate was probably finished by 1512.

THE SIXTEENTH-CENTURY REBUILDING

Significant damage, however, was done in 1513 when the castle was captured by a Scots army equipped with an impressive siege train with newly acquired bronze guns. The Outer Ward fell after just two days of bombardment and part of the Great Tower was brought down. In less than three weeks, Norham was again in the Bishop of Durham's hands following the English victory over the Scots at the Battle of Flodden nearby. Repairs began with some urgency and much

of the castle that can be seen today must be of this date. Between 1513–15 the Great Tower was re-roofed and Clapham's Tower (named after the Captain of the castle at the time) was built. By 1518–21, the Inner Ward was said to be finished, as was the long wall from the West Gate to the Inner Ward which was ready for its battlements. The Outer Ward was still weak, but in 1521, Thomas, Lord Dacre, deputy captain, reported that the Inner Ward was of such strength that, 'with the help of God and the prayer of St Cuthbert it is unprignable'. In September 1523, the Earl of Surrey added to the castle's defences and sent for expert gunners from Portsmouth. There was a garrison at this point of 20 gunners, 70 archers, 100 horsemen and, '7 or 8 countrymen for watchers'. Yet in 1526 there was a request for urgent repairs: 'for there is not a house in it that keeps out the rain. No part of the Outer Ward is finished as it should be except one gatehouse, nor is there half enough ordnance even if it were all serviceable'.

The rebuilding which followed the siege of 1513 produced drastic changes to the old-style medieval form of defence. This now involved providing for cannon and handguns in a systematic way. Clapham's Tower was part of this process, as well as the four towers or bulwarks on the south side of the outer ward and the casemates in the north-west curtain.

Guns were also mounted on top of the Great Tower and on the flat roof of the rebuilt hall. Yet, from contemporary accounts, it seems that progress on the Outer Ward was always slow. The Earl of Surrey built 'dyvers platformys rampires and [mended] broken places with turvis and yerthe' against the possibility of siege in 1523, which suggests emergency measures. In 1545, the King's Council ordered the strengthening of weak places at the castle, but responsibility for it was still the bishop's. This changed in 1559 when Bishop Tunstall refused to take the Oath of Supremacy, and the whole of Norhamshire, including its castle, was taken from him and passed into the possession of Queen Elizabeth I.

The remains of Clapham's Tower in the foreground. Behind it is the Great Tower, built in 1515 as a fortification in which to mount artillery

In 1542, Sir Robert Bowes, in his Survey of the Borders, reported that Norham was in good condition both in repairs and fortifications and 'stuffed with artyllery'. Nine years later, however, came a damning report also by Sir Robert Bowes. The Inner Ward was 'in no place flanked save by a little bulwarke or casamata' (Clapham's Tower) whose own pointed angle was not covered. One half of the dungeon (Great Tower) had fallen long before. The Outer Ward was enclosed by a very old wall that was thin and weak except for sundry little towers, 'which were not ingenyously devised'. In 1561, the military engineer, Rowland Johnson, was sent across from Berwick to inspect the castle's condition, and his report indicated much decay through lack of maintenance. 'Haulf of the donjon cleane downe to the vaultes' was in decay, although the other half was 60 feet high with guns mounted on the roof. The smaller towers were only fit for 'harquebusses' (hand guns). Only the Sheep Gate was in reasonable repair but it too had only 'a Lytle hole for a harquebusse'. Johnson's advice was that it would be better for a new fort to be built

A medieval leather knife scabbard found during excavation when the castle was taken into the guardianship of the state

nearby, properly flanked in the up-to-date manner. His accompanying plan of the castle shows how the occupied buildings were now largely confined to the Inner Ward which was now approached from the Sheep Gate.

The Outer Ward looks deserted apart from two long stable buildings. Johnson's plan is interesting because alongside it is an outline of the castle with a scheme superimposed over it showing an up-to-date artillery fort with eared bastions, similar to those that had been recently built at Berwick. The proposal shows how far advances in artillery fortification had changed military architecture.

In 1569, the castle was condemned as unfit for a garrison to live in, but in 1584 Norham was included in a survey of fifteen important castles and towers in the North. By 1594 it was so ruined that the only serviceable areas were two rooms in the gatehouse for the constable, and stabling for four horses. Even if the dismounted ordnance still in the castle were repaired, no 'conveniente platformees for them' existed any more. Two years later the Queen decided that she would spend no more on the castle. On Queen Elizabeth's death in 1603,

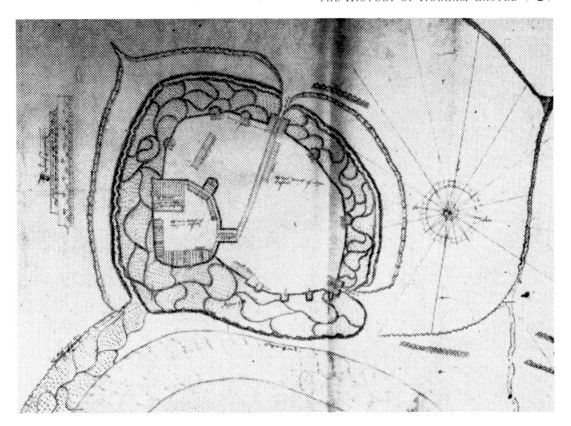

James VI of Scotland also became James I of England and the Tweed therefore ceased to exist as a frontier.

The ruins passed through many owners until 1923, when they were placed in the guardianship of the State. Excavation of the inner moat and clearance of fallen masonry was carried out, as well as consolidation of the ruins by the Office of Works. Since 1984, the castle has been cared for by English Heritage.

References

1. Philip Dixon and Pamela Marshall: 'The Great Tower in the Twelfth Century: The Case of Norham Castle', *The Archaeological Journal*, 150 (1993) pp.410–32.

Plan of Norham Castle, drawn by the military engineer, Rowland Johnson, in 1561

NORHAM CASTLE SITE PLAN

N

■	12th Century
■	Later medieval
□	16th Century
■	Modern

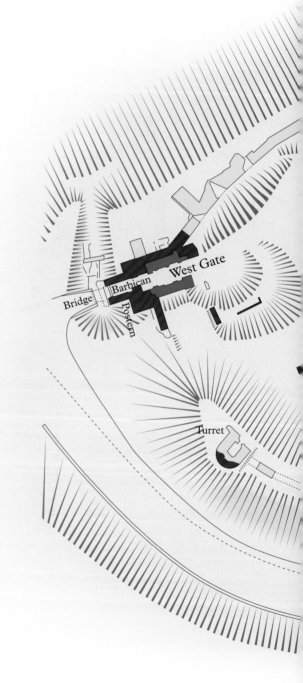

Bridge

Barbican

Postern

West Gate

Turret

0   *40 Metres*

0   *150 Feet*